THE BEST 50

BISCOTTI RECIPES

Barbara Karoff

BRISTOL PUBLISHING ENTERPRISES
San Leandro, California

Printed in the United States of America.

ISBN 1-55867-129-3

Cover design: Paredes Design Associates
Cover photography: John A. Benson
Food stylist: Suzanne Carreiro

ABOUT BISCOTTI

The only thing new about biscotti is how popular they are today. The term *biscotti* is the plural of *biscotto*, which can be roughly translated as "twice" (*bis*) + "cooked" (*cotto*).

Biscotti, and the smaller versions called *biscottini*, are the extra-crisp cookie slices that have taken America by storm. Italians have dunked these special twice-baked cookies in their coffee and wine since the fourteenth century. Now, in the eclectic 1990s, the American coffee house has embraced this time-honored tradition with passion. New and exotic flavor combinations now compete with the more standard and familiar.

Although Italians have been turning out biscotti since the Renaissance, very similar twice-baked cookies have developed in other countries as well. When long sea voyages became the norm in the sixteenth century, Columbus carried a form of biscotti, albeit a very plain one, in his ship's stores. English mariners packed barrels of a similar staple on their vessels. They called it *hard tack*. *Mandelbrot*, meaning "almond bread" in Yiddish, has a long tradition in Jewish cooking. Many versions are made with oil instead of butter, to conform with dietary laws. Today a number of varieties are studded with nuts other than almonds. The Dutch love their *rusk* and the Germans their *zwieback*. Both are variations on the twice-baked theme. The Greeks make a twice-baked cookie called *paxemadia* and the Spanish make one called *carquinyoles*.

Because biscotti are often not very sweet, they are perfect for enjoying throughout the day, from early breakfast to midnight snack. They complement coffee, tea, milk, hot chocolate, wine, fruit juice, fruit, ice cream and puddings. They are perfect for packing in lunch boxes and backpacks, are a first choice for picnics and they travel well in the mail. Most versions are low in both fat and sugar, and some contain no fat at all — except for the almost ever-present nuts.

Basic twice-baked biscotti are very simple cookies to make. They conveniently require few ingredients and no special equipment. They are quickly put together and they keep well.

Since the word biscotti is the generic Italian word for cookie, a number of other Italian cookie (biscotti) recipes are included in this collection. In this category, many readers will immediately recognize *Amaretti Cookies*, page 64, as the delightfully familiar (and expensive) melt-in-your-mouth confections sold in Italian delis and gourmet specialty stores as "Amarettini di Saronno." A close inspection of the distinctive red and orange tin identifies them as "biscotti." *St. Joseph's Cream Puffs*, page 72, those luscious ricotta-filled morsels, are another treat familiar to anyone who has visited an Italian bakery or been invited to celebrate in an Italian home.

HELPFUL HINTS

- In recipes calling for butter, margarine can be substituted, although it will, of course, produce a different flavor.
- Nuts are important to biscotti and few versions, however inven-

tive, are complete without one of the many nut varieties. Always toast the nuts before adding to the dough. Spread the nuts in a single layer in a shallow pan and place them in a 350°F oven for 8 to 10 minutes. Watch them carefully so they do not burn. Always cool the nuts completely before adding them to biscotti.

- If the dough is too sticky to handle when it is time to form it into logs, chill it in the refrigerator for 1 or 2 hours and then work it into logs on a well-floured surface.
- Form the dough into thin or fat logs. The cookies can be cut into thin or thick slices. The dough can be flattened on the baking sheet to a thickness of about ¾ inch and then cut into strips, squares or diamonds before the second baking.
- Line baking sheets with parchment paper (available in many supermarkets and in gourmet specialty stores) or spray them with nonstick cooking spray. Parchment paper eliminates pan cleanup and can be reused several times.

- Do not crowd the biscotti slices on the baking sheet for the second baking. They need room for the hot air to circulate.
- Always allow the biscotti logs to cool on a rack for at least 5 minutes before slicing, and always cool biscotti completely on a rack before storing.
- Use a very sharp knife, preferably a serrated one, to slice biscotti.
- Biscotti become more crisp as they cool, so take that into consideration when timing the second baking. Also, ovens vary and so do preferences. It's best to err on the side of not-too-dry, as biscotti can always be placed back in the oven for a few minutes to re-crisp or to add more crunch, if desired.
- Store biscotti in airtight containers; they pick up moisture easily.
- Because they keep well, it is practical to prepare a batch of biscotti when you have some free time. They are ideal for many occasions. All recipes in this book can be doubled successfully.

ANISE ALMOND BISCOTTI

These are the perfect biscotti to serve with a glass of wine.

1 cup sugar
1 cup coarsely chopped toasted almonds
½ cup butter, melted
2 tbs. crushed anise seeds
1 tbs. anise extract
1 tbs. water
1 tsp. vanilla extract
3 medium eggs
2¾ cups all-purpose flour
½ tbs. baking powder

In a large bowl, combine sugar, almonds, butter, anise seeds, anise extract, water and vanilla. Beat in eggs, one at a time. In a medium bowl, combine flour and baking powder and stir into anise mixture. Cover and refrigerate for 3 hours. Divide dough in halves or thirds. On a well-floured surface, shape into logs. Transfer logs to a parchment paper-lined or lightly sprayed baking sheet, and bake in a preheated 375° oven for 20 minutes or until firm and lightly browned. Cool on a rack for at least 5 minutes. Cut logs on the diagonal into ¾-inch slices. Return slices to baking sheet, leaving space around each slice, and continue baking for 15 minutes or until desired crispness. Cool completely on rack.

Makes 36

TUSCAN SPICE AND ALMOND BISCOTTI

Cinnamon, allspice and almonds are a fine flavor combination.

1 cup toasted almonds
1 cup plus 2 tbs. all-purpose flour
¼ tsp. baking powder
¼ tsp. baking soda
¼ tsp. salt
¼ tsp. cinnamon
¼ tsp. allspice
⅓ cup sugar
¼ cup butter, softened
2 tbs. honey
1 medium egg
½ tsp. vanilla extract
¼ tsp. almond extract

In a food processor or blender, finely grind ⅓ of the almonds. In a bowl, combine ground almonds, flour, baking powder, soda, salt, cinnamon and allspice. In a large bowl, cream sugar and butter. Mix in honey, egg, vanilla and almond extract. Gradually blend in dry mixture and remaining almonds. Divide dough in halves or thirds. On a well-floured surface, shape into logs. Transfer logs to a parchment paper-lined or lightly sprayed baking sheet, and bake in a preheated 350° oven for 20 minutes or until firm and lightly browned. Cool on a rack for at least 5 minutes. Cut logs on the diagonal into ¾-inch slices. Return slices to baking sheet, leaving space around each slice, and continue baking for 10 to 15 minutes or until desired crispness. Cool completely on rack.

Makes 36

CINNAMON ALMOND RAISIN BISCOTTI

Ground almonds add richness to these biscotti.

1 cup toasted almonds
½ cup brown sugar, firmly packed
¼ cup butter, softened
2 medium eggs
1 tsp. vanilla extract
1 tsp. almond extract
1 cup coarsely chopped toasted almonds
1 cup golden raisins
1½ cups all-purpose flour
1½ tsp. cinnamon
¾ tsp. baking powder

In a blender or food processor, grind 1 cup almonds with brown sugar. In a large bowl, cream butter with almond mixture. Stir in eggs, vanilla, almond extract, chopped almonds and raisins. In a medium bowl, combine flour, cinnamon and baking powder; add to almond mixture. Divide dough in halves or thirds. On a well-floured surface, shape into logs. Transfer logs to a parchment paper-lined or lightly sprayed baking sheet, and bake in a preheated 350° oven for 15 to 20 minutes or until firm and lightly browned. Cool on a rack for at least 5 minutes. Cut logs on the diagonal into ¾-inch slices. Return slices to baking sheet, leaving space around each slice, and continue baking for 10 minutes or until desired crispness. Cool completely on rack.

Makes 24

ALMOND BISCOTTI

These basic biscotti are always delicious.

1 cup all-purpose flour	2 medium eggs
½ cup sugar	½ tsp. vanilla extract
½ tsp. baking soda	½ tsp. almond extract
pinch salt	1 cup toasted almonds

In a bowl, combine flour, sugar, soda and salt. In another bowl, whisk together eggs, vanilla and almond extract; stir into dry ingredients. Add almonds. Divide dough in halves or thirds. On a well-floured surface, shape into logs. Transfer logs to a parchment paper-lined or lightly sprayed baking sheet, and bake in a preheated 300° oven for 30 minutes or until firm and lightly browned. Cool on a rack for at least 5 minutes. Cut logs on the diagonal into ¾-inch slices. Return slices to baking sheet, leaving space around each slice, and continue baking for 15 minutes or until desired crispness. Cool completely on rack.

Makes 24

RUM MACADAMIA NUT BISCOTTI

Rum and macadamia nuts make these biscotti special.

1 cup sugar
½ cup butter, softened
2 tbs. dark rum
4 medium eggs

3 cups all-purpose flour
1½ tsp. baking powder
3 cups coarsely chopped
    toasted macadamia nuts

In a bowl, cream sugar and butter. Add rum and eggs; mix well. In another bowl, combine flour and baking powder; stir into rum mixture. Add nuts. Divide dough in halves or thirds. On a well-floured surface, shape into logs. Transfer logs to a parchment paper-lined or lightly sprayed baking sheet; bake in a preheated 350° oven for 20 minutes or until firm and lightly browned. Cool on a rack for at least 5 minutes. Cut logs on the diagonal into ¾-inch slices. Return slices to baking sheet, leaving space around each slice; continue baking for 15 to 20 minutes or until desired crispness. Cool completely on rack.

Makes 48

HAZELNUT APRICOT BISCOTTI

Ground hazelnuts give these biscotti an extra-rich flavor.

1 cup sugar
½ cup butter, softened
2 tsp. vanilla extract
4 medium eggs
1 cup finely ground hazelnuts
3 cups all-purpose flour
1½ tsp. baking powder
1½ cups coarsely chopped toasted hazelnuts
1½ cups coarsely chopped dried apricots

In a large bowl, cream sugar and butter. Add vanilla, eggs and ground hazelnuts. In a medium bowl, combine flour and baking powder and add to ground hazelnut mixture. Stir in chopped hazelnuts and apricots. Divide dough in halves or thirds. On a well-floured surface, shape into logs. Transfer logs to a parchment paper-lined or lightly sprayed baking sheet, and bake in a preheated 350° oven for 20 minutes or until firm and lightly browned. Cool on a rack for at least 5 minutes. Cut logs on the diagonal into ¾-inch slices. Return slices to baking sheet, leaving space around each slice, and continue baking for 10 to 15 minutes or until desired crispness. Cool completely on rack.

Makes 48

MAPLE PECAN BISCOTTI

Maple adds its distinctive flavor to these crisp biscotti.

½ cup brown sugar,
  firmly packed
¼ cup butter, softened
2 tbs. maple extract

2 medium eggs
2 cups toasted pecans
1½ cups all-purpose flour
¾ tsp. baking powder

In a bowl, cream sugar and butter. Add maple extract, eggs and pecans. In a medium bowl, combine flour and baking powder; add to pecan mixture. Divide dough in halves or thirds. On a well-floured surface, shape into logs. Transfer logs to a parchment paper-lined or lightly sprayed baking sheet; bake in a preheated 350° oven for 15 to 20 minutes or until firm and lightly browned. Cool on a rack for at least 5 minutes. Cut logs on the diagonal into ¾-inch slices. Return slices to baking sheet, leaving space around each slice, and continue baking for 10 to 15 minutes or until desired crispness. Cool completely on rack.

Makes 24

PUMPKIN PECAN BISCOTTI

Add this pumpkin treat to your Thanksgivin

½ cup sugar
¼ cup butter, softened
2 medium eggs
½ cup canned pumpkin
1½ cups toasted pecans

1½ cups all-p
1 tsp. cinnamon
½ tsp. freshly grated nutmeg
½ tsp. ground cloves
¾ tsp. baking powder

In a bowl, cream sugar and butter. Stir in eggs, pumpkin and nuts; mix well. In another bowl, combine remaining ingredients; add to nut mixture. Divide dough in halves or thirds. On a well-floured surface, shape into logs; transfer to a parchment paper-lined or lightly sprayed baking sheet; bake in a preheated 350° oven for 15 to 20 minutes or until firm and lightly browned. Cool on a rack for at least 5 minutes. Cut logs on the diagonal into ¾-inch slices; return to baking sheet, leaving space around each slice, and continue baking for 10 to 15 minutes or until desired crispness. Cool completely on rack.

Makes 24

TRIPLE GINGER PECAN BISCOTTI

These biscotti feature great flavor and the crunch of pecans.

/2 cup sugar
¼ cup butter, softened
2 tbs. ground ginger
1 tbs. grated ginger root
¾ cup minced crystallized ginger

2 medium eggs
1½ cups coarsely chopped
  toasted pecans
1½ cups all-purpose flour
¾ tsp. baking powder

In a bowl, cream sugar and butter. Stir in gingers, eggs and pecans. In a small bowl, combine flour and baking powder; add to ginger mixture. Divide dough in halves or thirds. On a well-floured surface, shape into logs. Transfer logs to a parchment paper-lined or lightly sprayed baking sheet; bake in a preheated 375° oven for 20 minutes or until firm and lightly browned. Cool on a rack for at least 5 minutes. Cut logs on the diagonal into ¾-inch slices. Return slices to baking sheet, leaving space around each slice; continue baking for 15 to 20 minutes or until desired crispness. Cool completely on rack.

Makes 24

SESAME ORANGE BISCOTTI

Sesame seeds are a pleasant surprise in these biscotti.

½ cup sugar
¼ cup butter, softened
1 tbs. grated orange peel
2 medium eggs

½ cup toasted sesame seeds
1½ cups all-purpose flour
¾ tsp. baking powder
1 tsp. cinnamon

In a bowl, combine sugar and butter. Stir in orange peel and eggs. Add sesame seeds. In another bowl, combine flour, baking powder and cinnamon; add to sesame seed mixture. Divide dough in halves or thirds. On a well-floured surface, shape into logs. Transfer logs to a parchment paper-lined or lightly sprayed baking sheet, and bake in a preheated 375° oven for 20 minutes or until firm and lightly browned. Cool on a rack for at least 5 minutes. Cut logs on the diagonal into ¾-inch slices. Return slices to baking sheet, leaving space around each slice, and continue baking for 10 to 15 minutes or until desired crispness. Cool completely on rack.

Makes 24

BURSTING-WITH-FRUIT BISCOTTI

These cake-like biscotti are filled with fruit and nuts.

½ cup golden raisins
⅔ cup dried cranberries
⅔ cup chopped dried apricots
¼ cup sherry
3 medium eggs, separated
1¼ cups sugar
½ cup butter, melted and cooled
2 tsp. vanilla extract
3 cups all-purpose flour
¾ tsp. baking powder
½ cup toasted pistachio nuts
½ cup toasted walnuts

In a small bowl, combine raisins, cranberries, apricots and sherry; set aside for 30 minutes. In a large bowl, beat egg yolks with half of the sugar. In another bowl, beat egg whites; add remaining sugar and continue beating until a soft meringue forms. Fold meringue into egg yolks.

In another bowl, combine several spoonfuls of meringue and egg yolks with butter and vanilla; add it back to meringue and egg yolks. In a medium bowl, combine flour and baking powder and add to meringue and egg yolks. Work in fruits with sherry, and nuts. Divide dough in halves or thirds. On a well-floured surface, shape into logs. Transfer logs to a parchment paper-lined or lightly sprayed baking sheet, and bake in a preheated 350° oven for 30 minutes or until firm and lightly browned. Cool on a rack for at least 5 minutes. Cut logs on the diagonal into ¾-inch slices. Return slices to baking sheet, leaving space around each slice, and continue baking for 10 to 15 minutes or until desired crispness. Cool completely on rack.

Makes 36

FIG LEMON ROSEMARY BISCOTTI

There's a hint of the Greek countryside in these flavorful biscotti.

1 cup sugar
½ cup butter, softened
1 tsp. almond extract
1 tsp. minced fresh rosemary
3 medium eggs
1 cup finely chopped dried figs
½ cup finely chopped candied lemon peel
½ cup toasted almonds
2¾ cups all-purpose flour
1½ tsp. baking powder

In a large bowl, cream sugar and butter. Stir in almond extract, rosemary and eggs. Add figs, lemon peel and nuts. In a medium bowl, combine flour and baking powder and add to fruit-nut mixture. Cover and refrigerate for 3 hours. Divide dough in halves or thirds. On a well-floured surface, shape into logs. Transfer logs to a parchment paper-lined or lightly sprayed baking sheet, and bake in a preheated 375° oven for 20 minutes or until firm and lightly browned. Cool on a rack for at least 5 minutes. Cut logs on the diagonal into ¾-inch slices. Return slices to baking sheet, leaving space around each slice, and continue baking for 15 minutes or until desired crispness. Cool completely on rack.

Makes 48

LEMON GINGER BISCOTTI

With lots of ginger and nuts, these biscotti are perfect for dessert.

½ cup sugar
¼ cup butter, softened
1 tsp. vanilla extract
1 tsp. lemon extract
1 tsp. grated lemon peel
2 medium eggs
1 cup coarsely chopped crystallized ginger
1 cup toasted walnuts
1½ cups all-purpose flour
¾ tsp. baking powder
½ tsp. ground ginger

In a large bowl, cream sugar and butter. Add vanilla, lemon extract, lemon peel and eggs. Stir in crystallized ginger and nuts. In a medium bowl, combine flour, baking powder and ground ginger; add to lemon mixture. Divide dough in halves or thirds. On a well-floured surface, shape into logs. Transfer logs to a parchment paper-lined or lightly sprayed baking sheet, and bake in a preheated 350° oven for 15 to 20 minutes or until firm and lightly browned. Cool on a rack for at least 5 minutes. Cut logs on the diagonal into ¾-inch slices. Return slices to baking sheet, leaving space around each slice, and continue baking for 10 to 15 minutes or until desired crispness. Cool completely on rack.

Makes 24

TASTE-OF-THE-TROPICS BISCOTTI

The luscious taste of the tropics makes these biscotti special.

½ cup sugar
¼ cup butter, softened
2 medium eggs
1 cup chopped dried pineapple soaked in ¼ cup rum
½ cup unsweetened coconut
½ cup coarsely chopped toasted Brazil nuts
2 cups all-purpose flour
¾ tsp. baking powder

In a large bowl, cream sugar and butter. Add eggs and combine well. Add pineapple and soaking liquid, coconut and nuts. In a medium bowl, combine flour and baking powder and add to pineapple mixture. Divide dough in halves or thirds. On a well-floured surface, shape into logs. Transfer logs to a parchment paper-lined or lightly sprayed baking sheet, and bake in a preheated 375° oven for 20 minutes or until firm and lightly browned. Cool on a rack for at least 5 minutes. Cut logs on the diagonal into ¾-inch slices. Return slices to baking sheet, leaving space around each slice, and continue baking for 15 minutes or until desired crispness. Cool completely on rack.

Makes 24

NO-GUILT BISCOTTI

These biscotti contain so many good-for-you ingredients!

½ cup bran
½ cup rolled oats
1 cup all-purpose flour
½ cup whole wheat flour
½ cup brown sugar, firmly packed
1 tsp. baking powder
1 tsp. cinnamon
2 large eggs
¼ cup honey
1 tsp. vanilla extract
⅔ cup finely chopped mixed dried fruit
½ cup toasted pecans

In a large bowl, combine bran, oats, flours, brown sugar, baking powder and cinnamon. In a small bowl, whisk eggs, honey and vanilla; add to dry ingredients. Work in fruits and nuts. Divide dough in halves or thirds. On a well-floured surface, shape into logs. Transfer logs to a parchment paper-lined or lightly sprayed baking sheet, and bake in a preheated 325° oven for 20 to 25 minutes or until firm and lightly browned. Cool on a rack for at least 5 minutes. Reduce heat to 300°. Cut logs on the diagonal into ¾-inch slices. Return slices to baking sheet, leaving space around each slice, and continue baking for 15 minutes or until desired crispness. Cool completely on rack.

Makes 24

CASHEW ORANGE CRUNCH BISCOTTI

A wonderful orange flavor permeates these nutty biscotti.

1¼ cups all-purpose flour
½ cup sugar
½ tsp. baking soda
pinch salt

2 medium eggs
2 tbs. grated orange peel
1 cup toasted cashews

In a bowl, combine flour, sugar, soda and salt. In a small bowl, whisk eggs with orange peel. Stir into dry ingredients, add cashews and mix well. Divide dough in halves or thirds. On a well-floured surface, shape into logs. Transfer logs to a parchment paper-lined or lightly sprayed baking sheet; bake in a preheated 300° oven for 20 minutes or until firm and lightly browned. Cool on a rack for at least 5 minutes. Cut logs on the diagonal into ¾-inch slices. Return slices to baking sheet, leaving space around each slice, and continue baking for 15 minutes or until desired crispness. Cool completely on rack.

Makes 24

LEMON POPPY SEED BISCOTTI

Poppy seeds and tangy lemon give these biscotti special appeal.

1 cup sugar
½ cup butter, softened
3 medium eggs
2 tbs. poppy seeds
½ tsp. lemon extract

1 tbs. grated lemon peel
3 cups all-purpose flour
1½ tsp. baking powder
pinch salt

In a bowl, cream sugar and butter. Add eggs, poppy seeds, and lemon extract and peel. In another bowl, combine remaining ingredients; add to lemon mixture. Divide dough in halves or thirds. On a well-floured surface, shape into logs; transfer to a parchment paper-lined or lightly sprayed baking sheet. Bake in a preheated 375° oven for 20 minutes or until firm and lightly browned. Cool on a rack for at least 5 minutes. Cut logs on the diagonal into ¾-inch slices. Return slices to baking sheet, leaving space around each slice, and continue baking for 10 minutes or until firm and lightly browned. Cool completely on rack.

Makes 48

FIG PISTACHIO BISCOTTI

Figs and pistachios are an exotic and winning combination.

½ cup sugar
¼ cup butter, softened
2 medium eggs
1 tsp. vanilla extract
1 tsp. lemon extract

1 cup unsalted toasted pistachio nuts
1 cup chopped dried figs
1½ cups all-purpose flour
¾ tsp. baking powder

In a bowl, cream sugar and butter; stir in eggs, and vanilla and lemon extracts. Add pistachios and figs. In another bowl, combine flour and baking powder; add to fig mixture. Divide dough in halves or thirds. On a well-floured surface, shape into logs; transfer to a parchment paper-lined or lightly sprayed baking sheet, and bake in a preheated 350° oven for 15 to 20 minutes or until firm and lightly browned. Cool on a rack for at least 5 minutes. Cut logs on the diagonal into ¾-inch slices; return to baking sheet, leaving space around each slice; continue baking for 10 to 15 minutes or until desired crispness. Cool completely on rack.

Makes 24

CRANBERRY ORANGE BISCOTTI

Cranberry and orange are a festive holiday flavor combination.

1 cup sugar
½ cup butter, softened
1 tsp. orange extract
2 tbs. grated orange peel
4 medium eggs

3 cups all-purpose flour
1½ tsp. baking powder
2 cups dried cranberries
1 cup coarsely chopped toasted
  walnuts

In a bowl, cream sugar and butter. Add orange extract and peel, and eggs; mix well. In another bowl, combine flour and baking powder; add to orange mixture. Stir in cranberries and nuts. Divide dough in halves or thirds. On a well-floured surface, shape into logs; transfer to a parchment paper-lined or lightly oiled baking sheet, and bake in a preheated 350° oven for 20 minutes or until firm and lightly browned. Cool on a rack for at least 5 minutes. Cut logs on the diagonal into ¾-inch slices; return to baking sheet, leaving space around each slice, and continue baking for 15 minutes or until desired crispness. Cool completely on rack.

Makes 48

MINCEMEAT WALNUT BISCOTTI

These biscotti are too good to save for Christmas.

²⁄₃ cup crumbled condensed mincemeat
¹⁄₄ cup brandy
¹⁄₂ cup sugar
¹⁄₄ cup butter, softened
2 medium eggs
1¹⁄₂ cups coarsely chopped toasted walnuts
1¹⁄₂ cups all-purpose flour
³⁄₄ tsp. baking powder

In a small bowl, combine mincemeat and brandy; set aside. In another bowl, cream sugar and butter. Add eggs and mix well. Add mincemeat mixture. Stir in nuts. In another bowl, combine flour and baking powder and add to mincemeat mixture. Divide dough in halves or thirds. On a well-floured surface, shape into logs. Transfer logs to a parchment paper-lined or lightly sprayed baking sheet, and bake in a preheated 350° oven for 10 to 15 minutes or until firm and lightly browned. Cool on a rack for at least 5 minutes. Cut logs on the diagonal into ¾-inch slices. Return slices to baking sheet, leaving space around each slice, and continue baking for 10 to 15 minutes or until desired crispness. Cool completely on rack.

Makes 24

CHOCOLATE-DIPPED ORANGE BISCOTTI

These biscotti make the most of the ever-popular chocolate and orange flavor combination.

1 cup sugar
½ cup butter, softened
2 tsp. orange extract
2 tbs. grated orange peel
4 medium eggs
3 cups all-purpose flour
1½ tsp. baking powder
2 cups coarsely chopped toasted walnuts
1 cup bittersweet chocolate chips, melted

In a large bowl, cream sugar and butter. Add orange extract, orange peel and eggs. In a medium bowl, combine flour and baking powder and stir into orange mixture. Add nuts. Divide dough in halves or thirds. On a well-floured surface, shape into logs. Transfer logs to a parchment paper-lined or lightly sprayed baking sheet, and bake in a preheated 350° oven for 15 minutes or until firm and lightly browned. Cool on a rack for at least 5 minutes. Cut logs on the diagonal into ¾-inch slices. Return slices to baking sheet, leaving space around each slice, and continue baking for 10 to 15 minutes or until desired crispness. Place on rack and, when completely cooled, dip about ⅓ of each biscotti into melted chocolate. Dry on rack.

Makes 48

CHOCOLATE-MARMALADE BISCOTTI

*Seville orange marmalade, which is not too sweet,
is best in this recipe.*

²⁄₃ cup sugar
¹⁄₃ cup butter, softened
2 medium eggs
3 tbs. Seville orange marmalade
2 tbs. grated orange peel
2¹⁄₃ cups all-purpose flour
1¹⁄₂ tsp. baking powder
pinch salt
¹⁄₂ cup toasted walnuts
³⁄₄ cup milk chocolate chips

In a large bowl, cream sugar and butter. Beat in eggs, marmalade and orange peel. In a medium bowl, combine flour, baking powder and salt; add to marmalade mixture. Blend in nuts and chocolate chips. Divide dough in halves or thirds. On a well-floured surface, shape into logs. Transfer logs to a parchment paper-lined or lightly sprayed baking sheet, and bake in a preheated 325° oven for 25 minutes or until firm and lightly browned. Cool on a rack for at least 5 minutes. Cut logs on the diagonal into ¾-inch slices. Return slices to baking sheet, leaving space around each slice, and continue baking for 10 minutes or until desired crispness. Cool completely on rack.

Makes 42

MILK CHOCOLATE AND HONEY BISCOTTI

These biscotti are especially good with a big glass of milk.

½ cup honey
¼ cup butter, softened
1 tsp. vanilla extract
2 medium eggs

1½ cups coarsely chopped
  milk chocolate
2 cups all-purpose flour
1 tbs. baking powder

In a bowl, combine honey, butter, vanilla and eggs. Stir in chocolate. In another bowl, combine flour and baking powder; add to chocolate mixture. Divide dough in halves or thirds. On a well-floured surface, shape into logs. Transfer logs to a parchment paper-lined or lightly sprayed baking sheet, and bake in a preheated 350° oven for 15 to 20 minutes. Cool on a rack for at least 5 minutes. Cut logs on the diagonal into ¾-inch slices. Return slices to baking sheet, leaving space around each slice; continue baking for 10 to 15 minutes. Cool completely on rack.

Makes 24

CHOCK-FULL-OF-CHOCOLATE BISCOTTI

Two types of chocolate make these biscotti a delight.

½ cup toasted almonds
2½ cups all-purpose flour
¾ cup sugar
pinch salt

1 tsp. baking soda
3 large eggs, lightly beaten
½ cup milk chocolate chips
½ cup white chocolate chips

In a food processor or blender, grind almonds to a fine meal. In a bowl, combine almonds, flour, sugar, salt and soda. Stir in eggs. Place dough on a lightly floured surface. Knead to blend well and work in chips. Divide dough in halves or thirds. On a well-floured surface, shape into logs. Transfer logs to a parchment paper-lined or lightly sprayed baking sheet, and bake in a preheated 375° oven for 20 minutes or until firm and lightly browned. Cool on a rack for at least 5 minutes. Cut logs on the diagonal into ¾-inch slices. Return slices to baking sheet, leaving space around each slice, and continue baking for 20 minutes. Cool completely on rack.

Makes 36

COCONUT BISCOTTI DIPPED IN CHOCOLATE

Coconut and chocolate are a well-loved flavor combination.

½ cup sugar
½ cup butter, softened
2 tbs. vanilla extract
2 medium eggs
1½ cups unsweetened coconut
1½ cups all-purpose flour
¾ tsp. baking powder
½ cup bittersweet chocolate chips, melted

In a large bowl, cream sugar and butter. Add vanilla, eggs and coconut. In a medium bowl, combine flour and baking powder and stir into coconut mixture. Divide dough in halves or thirds. On a well-floured surface, shape into logs. Transfer logs to a parchment paper-lined or lightly sprayed baking sheet, and bake in a preheated 350° oven for 15 to 20 minutes or until firm and lightly browned. Cool on a rack for at least 5 minutes. Cut logs on the diagonal into ¾-inch slices. Return slices to baking sheet, leaving space around each slice, and continue baking for 10 to 15 minutes or until desired crispness. Place on rack and, when completely cooled, dip about ⅓ of each biscotti into melted chocolate. Dry on rack.

Makes 24

CHOCOLATY CHOCOLATE BISCOTTI
DIPPED IN CHOCOLATE

This is a biscotti made to order for chocolate lovers.

½ cup sugar
¼ cup butter, softened
1 tbs. chocolate extract
2 medium eggs
1 cup bittersweet chocolate chips
1½ cups all-purpose flour
¾ tsp. baking powder
½ cup white chocolate chips, melted

In a large bowl, cream sugar and butter. Stir in chocolate extract and eggs. Add bittersweet chocolate chips. In a medium bowl, combine flour and baking powder and add to chocolate mixture. Divide dough in halves or thirds. On a well-floured surface, shape into logs. Transfer logs to a parchment paper-lined or lightly sprayed baking sheet, and bake in a preheated 350° oven for 10 to 15 minutes or until firm and lightly browned. Cool on a rack for at least 5 minutes. Cut logs on the diagonal into ¾-inch slices. Return slices to baking sheet, leaving space around each slice, and continue baking for 10 minutes or until desired crispness. Cool completely on rack and, using a pastry brush, paint each biscotti on one side with melted white chocolate.

Makes 24

CHOCOLATE RASPBERRY BISCOTTI

Chocolate and raspberry are a magic flavor combination.

½ cup sugar
¼ cup butter, softened
1 medium egg
2 cups all-purpose flour
⅓ cup unsweetened cocoa powder
¾ tsp. baking powder
¾ cup raspberry jam

In a medium bowl, cream sugar and butter. Mix in egg. In a small bowl, combine flour, cocoa and baking powder; add to butter mixture. Stir in jam. Divide dough in halves or thirds. On a well-floured surface, shape into logs. Transfer logs to a parchment paper-lined or lightly sprayed baking sheet, and bake in a preheated 325° oven for 25 minutes or until firm and lightly browned. Cool on a rack for at least 5 minutes. Cut logs on the diagonal into ¾-inch slices. Return slices to baking sheet, leaving space around each slice, and continue baking for 10 to 15 minutes or until desired crispness. Cool completely on rack.

Makes 24

MOCHA BRAZIL NUT BISCOTTI

Watch the second baking carefully. These burn easily.

½ cup sugar
¼ cup butter, softened
1 tbs. chocolate extract
2 medium eggs
1 cup coarsely chopped
  toasted Brazil nuts

1⅓ cups all-purpose flour
1¼ tsp. baking powder
2 tbs. unsweetened cocoa
  powder
2 tbs. instant coffee powder

In a bowl, cream sugar and butter. Add chocolate extract and eggs; mix well. Add nuts. Combine remaining ingredients; add to egg mixture. Divide dough in halves or thirds. On a well-floured surface, shape into logs; transfer to a parchment paper-lined or lightly sprayed baking sheet; bake in a preheated 350° oven for 20 minutes or until firm. Cool on a rack for at least 5 minutes. Cut logs on the diagonal into ¾-inch slices; return to baking sheet, leaving space around each slice; continue baking for 10 to 15 minutes or until desired crispness. Cool completely on rack.

Makes 24

PEPPER AND PEANUT BISCOTTI

These biscotti have a peppery bite and are not very sweet.

¼ cup sugar
1½ tbs. butter, softened
2 large eggs
1 tbs. water
1 cup coarsely chopped salted peanuts, without skins
2 cups all-purpose flour
2 tsp. coarsely ground pepper
⅛ tsp. chili powder
1 tsp. baking powder
½ tsp. baking soda
1 tsp. salt

In a large bowl, cream sugar and butter. Add eggs and water and mix well. Stir in peanuts. In a medium bowl, combine flour, pepper, chili powder, baking powder, soda and salt; add to peanut mixture. Divide dough in halves or thirds. On a well-floured surface, shape into logs. Transfer logs to a parchment paper-lined or lightly sprayed baking sheet, and bake in a preheated 350° oven for 18 to 20 minutes or until firm and lightly browned. Cool on a rack for at least 5 minutes. Cut logs on the diagonal into ¾-inch slices. Return slices to baking sheet, leaving space around each slice, and continue baking for 15 to 20 minutes or until desired crispness. Cool completely on rack.

Makes 48

CORNMEAL PARMESAN BISCOTTI

*These biscotti are slightly savory, slightly sweet
and filled with good flavor.*

$\frac{1}{3}$ cup sugar
$\frac{1}{4}$ cup butter, softened
2 tbs. hot mustard
2 medium eggs
1 cup finely grated Parmesan cheese
$\frac{2}{3}$ cup toasted pumpkin seeds
1$\frac{1}{2}$ cups all-purpose flour
$\frac{1}{2}$ cup cornmeal
$\frac{3}{4}$ tsp. baking powder
pinch salt

In a large bowl, cream sugar and butter. Add mustard and eggs. Stir in Parmesan cheese and pumpkin seeds. In a medium bowl, combine flour, cornmeal, baking powder and salt; add to mustard mixture. If dough is too sticky, refrigerate for 1 to 2 hours. Divide dough in halves or thirds. On a well-floured surface, shape into logs. Transfer logs to a parchment paper-lined or lightly sprayed baking sheet, and bake in a preheated 375° oven for 20 minutes or until firm and lightly browned. Cool on a rack for at least 5 minutes. Cut logs on the diagonal into ³/₄-inch slices. Return slices to baking sheet, leaving space around each slice, and continue baking for 10 to 15 minutes or until desired crispness. Cool completely on rack.

Makes 24

CHILI CORN BISCOTTI

These savory biscotti are very crispy and are great with soups, salads and drinks.

1 cup frozen corn kernels, thawed
2 jalapeño chilies, deveined, seeded and minced
½ cup *plus* 3 tbs. all-purpose flour
⅓ cup finely grated cheddar cheese
¼ cup cornmeal
2 tbs. sugar
½ tsp. baking powder
½ tsp. salt
¼ tsp. baking soda
2 medium eggs

In a food processor or blender, coarsely chop corn. Do not puree. Transfer to a small bowl, stir in jalapeños and set aside. In a large bowl, combine flour, cheese, cornmeal, sugar, baking powder, salt and soda; stir in eggs. Add corn and jalapeños and mix well. Divide dough in halves or thirds. On a well-floured surface, shape into logs. Transfer logs to a parchment paper-lined or lightly sprayed baking sheet, and bake in a preheated 325° oven for 20 to 25 minutes or until firm and lightly browned. Cool on rack for at least 5 minutes. Cut logs on the diagonal into ¾-inch slices. Return slices to baking sheet, leaving space around each slice, and continue baking for 35 minutes or until desired crispness. Cool completely on rack.

Makes 18

CURRY PINE NUT BISCOTTI

These savory biscotti are nice with wine, soup or salad.

2 cups grated Parmesan cheese	3 cups all-purpose flour
½ cup butter, softened	1½ tsp. baking powder
4 medium eggs	3 tbs. curry powder
2 cups toasted pine nuts	1 tsp. salt

In a bowl, cream Parmesan and butter until well blended. Add eggs and stir in pine nuts. In another bowl, combine flour, baking powder, curry powder and salt; add to pine nut mixture. If dough is quite dry, mix with hands. Divide dough in halves or thirds. On a well-floured surface, shape into logs. Transfer logs to a parchment paper-lined or lightly sprayed baking sheet; bake in a preheated 375° oven for 20 minutes or until firm and lightly browned. Cool on a rack for at least 5 minutes. Cut logs on the diagonal into ¾-inch slices; return to baking sheet, leaving space around each slice, and continue baking for 20 minutes or until desired crispness. Cool completely on rack.

Makes 30

DUTCH WALNUT RUSKS

This is a very sticky dough. Use well-floured hands.

2 medium eggs
½ tsp. vanilla extract
¼ tsp. grated orange peel
⅔ cup sugar
1⅔ cups all-purpose flour

1 tsp. baking powder
pinch salt
¼ cup butter, softened
1 cup chopped toasted walnuts

In a bowl, combine eggs, vanilla, orange peel and sugar. In a small bowl, combine 1 cup flour, baking powder and salt; add to orange mixture. Beat in butter and remaining flour. Add walnuts. Divide dough in halves or thirds. On a well-floured surface, shape into logs. Transfer logs to a parchment paper-lined or lightly sprayed baking sheet, and bake in a preheated 325° oven for 25 minutes. Cool on a rack for at least 5 minutes. Cut logs on the diagonal into ¾-inch slices. Return slices to baking sheet, leaving space around each slice; continue baking for 15 minutes. Cool completely on rack.

Makes 36

GREEK PAXEMADIA

This is a Greek version of biscotti that originated as oven-dried slices of anise-flavored country bread.

1 cup sugar
¾ cup butter, softened
3 medium eggs
1 tbs. crushed coriander seeds
1 tbs. crushed anise seeds
2 tbs. grated orange peel
2 tbs. grated lemon peel
3 cups all-purpose flour
1½ tsp. baking powder
1½ cups coarsely chopped toasted walnuts

In a large bowl, cream sugar and butter. Add eggs. Mix in coriander and anise seeds and orange and lemon peels. In a medium bowl, combine flour and baking powder and stir into seed mixture. Add walnuts. Divide dough in halves or thirds. On a well-floured surface, shape into logs. Transfer logs to a parchment paper-lined or lightly sprayed baking sheet, and bake in a preheated 350° oven for 25 to 30 minutes or until firm and lightly browned. Cool on a rack for at least 5 minutes. Cut logs on the diagonal into ¾-inch slices. Return slices to baking sheet, leaving space around each slice, and continue baking for 10 minutes or until desired crispness. Cool completely on rack.

Makes 36

MILK CHOCOLATE WALNUT MANDELBROT

These Jewish cookies are dry, as they are supposed to be for dunking, but not as hard as many biscotti.

3½ cups all-purpose flour
2 tbs. baking powder
pinch salt
1 cup canola oil
1 cup sugar
3 medium eggs
1¼ cups coarsely chopped toasted walnuts
⅓ cup milk chocolate chips

Combine flour, baking powder and salt. In a large bowl, beat oil, sugar and eggs. Gradually stir in halves of the flour mixture. Fold in nuts, remaining flour and chocolate chips. Divide dough in halves or thirds. On a well-floured surface, shape into logs. Transfer logs to a parchment paper-lined or lightly sprayed baking sheet, and bake in a preheated 375° oven for 20 minutes or until firm and lightly browned. Cool on a rack for at least 5 minutes. Cut logs on the diagonal into ¾-inch slices. Return slices to baking sheet, leaving space around each slice, and continue baking for 15 minutes or until desired crispness. Cool completely on rack.

Makes 36

ROYAL DUNKERS

These cake-like, Ukrainian-style cookies are baked in a loaf pan.

1½ cups all-purpose flour
½ tsp. salt
1 tsp. baking powder
4 medium eggs
1 cup sugar

¼ cup canola oil
¼ cup frozen orange juice
   concentrate
2 tsp. vanilla extract
1 cup dried sour cherries

In a bowl, combine flour, salt and baking powder. In a medium bowl, beat eggs and sugar until fluffy. In another bowl, combine oil, orange juice concentrate and vanilla; stir into egg mixture alternately with flour mixture. Add cherries. Divide batter between 2 lightly sprayed 6-x-3-x-2-inch loaf pans, and bake in a preheated 350° oven for 30 minutes or until a toothpick inserted in the center comes out clean. Remove from pans, cool on a rack for 10 minutes and cut into ½-inch slices. Arrange slices on a baking sheet, leaving space around each slice; continue baking for 10 to 15 minutes. Cool completely on rack.

Makes 30

DOUBLE NUT COOKIES

Almonds and hazelnuts star in these wonderfully rich treats.

2 cups toasted almonds
2 large egg whites, lightly
  beaten
1 cup sugar

2 tbs. sherry, dark rum or fruit
  liqueur
1/3 cup finely chopped toasted
  hazelnuts

In a medium bowl, combine almonds and egg whites; stir to coat almonds. With a slotted spoon, remove nuts, reserving egg white, to a blender or food processor and blend to a smooth puree. Transfer to a bowl and stir in reserved egg whites, sugar and sherry to form a paste. Pinch off small portions of the dough and shape with hands into disks about 1½ inches in diameter. Press one side of each disk into hazelnuts and place on a parchment paper-lined baking sheet, nut side up. Allow to stand at room temperature for 2 hours. Bake in a preheated 400° oven for 5 to 8 minutes or until beginning to brown around the edges.

Makes 36

WINE DUNKERS

Delicious on their own, even better dunked in wine!

1 cup sugar
1/2 cup butter
2 tbs. anise seeds
2 tbs. anise liqueur (Anisette)
2 tbs. whiskey

1 cup almonds, toasted,
   coarsely chopped
3 eggs
2 3/4 cups all purpose flour,
   unsifted
1/2 tbs. baking powder

In a large bowl, cream sugar and butter. Add anise seeds, liqueur, whiskey and nuts. In another bowl, mix flour and baking powder and blend thoroughly into sugar mixture. Cover and chill 2-3 hours.

On lightly sprayed baking sheets, shape dough into flat loaves 1/2 inch thick, 2 inches wide and as long as the sheet. Place no more than 2 loaves, parallel and well apart, per sheet. Bake in preheated 375 oven for 20 minutes. Remove from oven and cool enough to handle. Cut in diagonal slices 1/2–3/4 inch thick. Return slices to sheets and continue baking at 375 for 15 minutes or until lightly toasted. Cool completely on racks.

Makes 48

BUSSOLAI

*These sweet crescents, a specialty of the Burano region
of Italy, are perfect with fruit and coffee.*

1¼ cups sugar
1 tbs. butter, softened
4 medium egg yolks

1 medium egg
1¾ cups all-purpose flour

In a large bowl, cream ¼ cup sugar and butter. Add remaining sugar and combine well. Stir in egg yolks and egg. Add flour and combine to form a stiff dough. Pinch off walnut-sized pieces, roll each into a cylinder and curve into a crescent. Place on a parchment paper-lined or lightly sprayed baking sheet, and bake in a preheated 350° oven for 15 to 20 minutes or until beginning to brown around the edges. Cool completely on a rack.

Makes 36

ITALIAN PINE NUT COOKIES

Pine nuts make these rich cookies especially attractive.

2 cups blanched almonds
2 medium egg whites, lightly beaten
1 cup sugar

2 tbs. orange juice concentrate
1 medium egg white, lightly beaten
¼ cup toasted pine nuts

Add almonds to 2 beaten egg whites and stir. With a slotted spoon, remove almonds to a blender or food processor and blend to a smooth paste. Transfer to a bowl and stir in sugar and orange juice concentrate. Shape dough into walnut-sized balls. Place on a parchment paper-lined or lightly sprayed baking sheet 1 inch apart and flatten to a ¼-inch thickness with the bottom of a glass. Brush tops with beaten egg white and stud with pine nuts in an attractive design. Allow to stand at room temperature for 2 hours. Bake in a preheated 400° oven for 5 to 8 minutes or until just beginning to brown around the edges. Cool completely on a rack.

Makes 36

AMARETTI COOKIES

*These are flat rather than the traditional round balls,
but otherwise they are the real thing.*

2 cups blanched almonds
1 cup sugar
1 tsp. almond extract

2 egg whites, stiffly beaten
confectioners' sugar for
  sprinkling

With a blender or food processor, finely grind almonds. Spread on a baking sheet and allow to dry in a slightly warm oven for several hours. In a medium bowl, combine almonds, sugar and almond extract. Fold in egg whites and blend thoroughly but gently. Spray and flour 2 baking sheets and drop batter by spoonfuls, leaving 2 inches between cookies. Sprinkle with confectioners' sugar and allow to stand at room temperature for 2 hours. Bake in a preheated 325° oven for 15 minutes or until golden. Cool on baking sheets for 2 minutes and remove to a rack to cool completely.

Makes 36

VENETIAN CORNMEAL COOKIES

These unusual cornmeal cookies are delightful with wine.

¾ cup golden raisins
⅔ cup rum
3 large egg yolks
¾ cup sugar
1 tsp. vanilla extract

grated peel of 1 lemon
1 cup butter, melted
1½ cups fine cornmeal
2 cups all-purpose flour
⅓ cup toasted pine nuts

In a bowl, combine raisins and rum and set aside. In a large bowl, whisk egg yolks, sugar and vanilla until smooth and thick. Stir in lemon peel and butter. In a medium bowl, combine cornmeal and flour and add to egg mixture. Drain raisins and save rum to use again. Add pine nuts and raisins. Break off walnut-sized pieces of dough, roll each into a ball and flatten to a ¼-inch thickness. Place on parchment paper-lined or lightly sprayed baking sheets; bake in a preheated 375° oven for 20 minutes or until beginning to brown. Cool on a rack.

Makes 48

WIDOW'S KISSES

*These light and airy meringue-like kisses
are completely delectable.*

4 large egg whites
½ cup plus 1 tbs. sugar
1 cup coarsely chopped toasted walnuts
¼ cup finely chopped citron

In the top of a double boiler over simmering water, beat egg whites and sugar until mixture is quite firm. Remove from hot water and stir in nuts and citron. Drop by spoonfuls onto a lightly sprayed baking sheet. Bake in a preheated 300° oven for 25 to 30 minutes or until lightly browned. Cool on baking sheet before removing to a rack.

Makes 24

SICILIAN HAZELNUT MERINGUES

These luscious meringues will melt in your mouth.

4 large egg whites
2½ cups confectioners' sugar
1 cup finely chopped toasted hazelnuts
grated peel of 1 orange

In a large bowl, beat egg whites until they form soft peaks. Gradually add sugar and continue beating until whites are very stiff. Fold in nuts and orange peel. Drop by spoonfuls onto a parchment paper-lined baking sheet, and bake in a preheated 350° oven for 30 minutes or until firm but still white. Cool on baking sheet.

Makes 18

QUEEN'S BISCUITS

These crisp cookies are called "Biscotti di Regina" in Italian.

1½ cups all-purpose flour
⅔ cup sugar
¾ tsp. baking powder
6 tbs. butter, melted
1 medium egg, lightly beaten

1 tsp. vanilla extract
2 tbs. grated orange peel
milk, as needed
¾ cup finely chopped toasted
 walnuts

In a large bowl, combine flour, sugar and baking powder. In a small bowl, whisk butter, egg, vanilla and orange peel; add to dry mixture. If dough is too dry, add milk, a teaspoon at a time, to make a workable dough. Pinch off small pieces of dough and form into cylinders about the size of your little finger. Roll each cylinder in chopped nuts to coat completely and place on a parchment paper-lined or lightly sprayed baking sheet. Bake in a preheated 350° oven for 15 minutes or until golden. Cool completely on a rack.

Makes 24

SICILIAN ALMOND AND CITRON COOKIES

*These simple and unusual cookies are
slightly chewy and not too sweet.*

¼ cup toasted almonds
⅓ cup sugar
2 cups all-purpose flour
1¼ tsp. baking powder

1 tsp. cinnamon
½ tsp. ground cloves
½ cup finely chopped citron
warm water, as needed

With a blender or food processor, blend almonds and sugar to a fine puree. In a bowl, combine almond puree, flour, baking powder, cinnamon, cloves and citron. Add enough warm water to make a firm dough and knead until elastic. On a well-floured surface, roll dough to a ½-inch thickness and cut into ½-inch strips. Place strips on a parchment paper-lined or lightly sprayed baking sheet and decorate in a crosshatch pattern with the tines of a fork. Bake in a preheated 400° oven for 10 to 15 minutes or until golden around the edges. Cool completely on a rack.

Makes 36

ITALIAN ORANGE COOKIES

These are called "Biscotti All' Arancio" in Italian.

1 cup sugar
4 medium eggs, room
  temperature

2 cups all-purpose flour
1 tbs. grated orange peel
sugar for sprinkling

In a medium bowl, beat ½ cup sugar and 2 eggs. Slowly add remaining sugar and continue beating. Add another egg and beat. Add remaining egg and beat until light and foamy. Fold in flour and orange peel. Drop by spoonfuls onto a parchment paper-lined or lightly sprayed baking sheet, making cookies as round as possible. Lightly sprinkle each cookie with sugar and allow to stand at room temperature for 3 hours. Bake in a preheated 350° oven for 10 minutes. Cool completely on a rack.

Makes 36

BISCOTTI ALLA VENENZIANA

These Venetian cookies are similar to flat, little sponge cakes.

5 medium eggs, separated
½ cup sugar
½ tbs. brandy

1 cup all-purpose flour
pinch salt
confectioners' sugar for sprinkling

In a large bowl, beat egg yolks and sugar until creamy. Add brandy. In a medium bowl, combine flour and salt and fold into egg yolk mixture. Beat egg whites until soft peaks form and stir ⅓ into flour mixture. When well combined, fold in remaining egg whites. Drop by spoonfuls onto a parchment paper-lined or lightly sprayed baking sheet, and bake in a preheated 350° oven for 10 minutes or until firm and beginning to brown around the edges. Cool completely on a rack and dust with confectioners' sugar when cold.

Makes 40

SARDINIAN HONEY CAKES

Make these little honey-flavored cookies in various shapes.

2 tbs. honey
1 tbs. butter
1 cup all-purpose flour
pinch salt

1 medium egg, lightly beaten
1 tsp. baking powder mixed
  with 1 tbs. milk

In a small saucepan, heat honey and butter, stirring until butter is melted and mixture is well blended. In a medium bowl, combine flour and salt. Add honey mixture, egg and baking powder mixed with milk. Mix to a smooth dough. On a lightly floured surface, roll dough to ⅛-inch thickness. Cut with cookie cutters. Place cookies on a parchment paper-lined or lightly sprayed baking sheet, and bake in a preheated 375° oven for 10 minutes or until brown around the edges. Cool completely on a rack.

Makes 24

ST. JOSEPH'S CREAM PUFFS

These are very popular Italian cookies — with good reason.

CREAM PUFF PASTE
1 cup hot water
½ cup butter
pinch salt
1 cup cake flour
4 medium eggs

FILLING
1 lb. ricotta cheese
⅓ cup chopped milk
chocolate chips
½ cup sugar
1 tbs. chopped candied orange peel
2 tbs. chopped toasted, unsalted pistachio nuts

To make cream puff paste: In a 2-quart saucepan, heat water, butter and salt to boiling. When butter is melted, lower heat and add flour, all at once. Stir with a wooden spoon until mixture leaves the sides of the pan. Remove from heat and cool to lukewarm. With a wooden spoon, beat in eggs, one at a time. Drop batter by spoonfuls onto a lightly sprayed baking sheet, leaving 2 inches between each puff. Bake in a preheated 450° oven for 10 minutes. Reduce heat to 300° and continue baking for 15 to 20 minutes. Cool completely on a rack.

To make filling: blend all ingredients.

Make slit in side of cooled puffs and fill. Refrigerate until ready to serve.

Makes 48

INDEX